"GIRL WITH WATERING CAN" AUGUSTE RENOIR
COURTESY OF THE NATIONAL GALLERY OF ART

COUSINS

Linda Chalmer Zemel

ISBN-10: 1492838187
ISBN-13: 9781492838180

For my grandchildren

with love from Grandma Linda

ABOUT THE AUTHOR

LINDA CHALMER ZEMEL received her BA and MA from the University of Rochester, where she also did doctoral work in human development.

She has been a News Book Reviewer for The Buffalo News and wrote and hosted a weekly radio interview program, "What's New," on WHLD AM in Buffalo. She also writes the Buffalo Books column and the Buffalo Alternative Medicine column for Examiner.com.

She is the author of a novel, *Witch Hunt*, and a stageplay, *Reunion*, as well as musical comedy and a book on dream theory.

She received the Excellence in Teaching Award from Rochester Institute of Technology College of Continuing Education, and received grant allocations for writing and performing in distance learning videos and for her work preparing teacher aides.

Currently, she lives in Western New York and teaches media writing and public speaking in the Communication Department at SUNY Buffalo State College.

Cousins are like brothers

That you don't know quite as well

WINSLOW HOMER "BREEZING UP (A FAIR WIND)"
COURTESY NATIONAL GALLERY OF ART, WASHINGTON

7

Never having lived with their socks.

EDOUARD MANET "THE OLD MUSICIAN"
COURTESY NATIONAL MUSEUM OF ART, WASHINGTON

Cousins are like sisters

That you don't know quite as well

CLAUDE MONET "WOMAN WITH A PARASOL"
COURTESY NATIONAL GALLERY OF ART, WASHINGTON

Never having shared their secrets.

EDOUARD MANET "THE RAILWAY"
COURTESY NATIONAL GALLERY OF ART, WASHINGTON

13

Cousins might have the same color hair.

They might be good at the same sport.

AUGUSTE RENOIR "PONT NEUF"
COURTESY NATIONAL GALLERY OF ART, WASHINGTON

They might all have the same color eyes.

They might all be good at math.

CLAUDE MONET "THE ARTIST'S GARDEN AT ARGENTEUIL"
COURTESY NATIONAL GALLERY OF ART, WASHINGTON

17

Sometimes their last name is the same as yours.

Sometimes it is different.

FOLLOWER OF PEETER GYSELS "RIVER LANDSCAPE WITH VILLAGES AND TRAVELERS"
COURTESY NATIONAL GALLERY OF ART, WASHINGTON

Cousins are friends

You know better than friends

CLAUDE MONET "STE. ADRESSE"
COURTESY NATIONAL GALLERY OF ART, WASHINGTON

21

Because your mom and their mom

Are sisters

EVA GONZALES "NANNY AND CHILD"
COURTESY NATIONAL GALLERY OF ART, WASHINGTON

Or your dad and their dad are brothers

CARIANI "A CONCERT"
COURTESY NATIONAL GALLERY OF ART, WASHINGTON

25

Or your mom and their dad

are sister and brother

CLAUDE MONET "BAZILLE AND CAMILLE (STUDY FOR "DEJEUNER SUR L'HERBE")"
COURTESY NATIONAL GALLERY OF ART, WASHINGTON

27

Or the other way around.

MARY CASSATT "THE BOATING PARTY"
COURTESY NATIONAL GALLERY OF ART, WASHINGTON

29

Their moms and dads

are your aunties and uncles.

"THE MUSIC LESSON"
COURTESY NATIONAL GALLERY OF ART, WASHINGTON

31

Cousins are the people you stay with

when your mom and dad go on a trip.

FOLLOWER OF JOHN SINCLAIR SARGENT "RESTING"
COURTESY NATIONAL GALLERY OF ART, WASHINGTON

33

Cousins are who

you celebrate with

HENRI DE TOULOUSE-LAUTREC "ALFRED LA GUIGNE"
COURTESY NATIONAL GALLERY OF ART, WASHINGTON

35

Like Thanksgiving dinners

and Chanukah parties

the fourth of July

and Passover Seders

and Easter.

AUGUSTE RENOIR "OARSMEN AT CHATOU"
COURTESY NATIONAL GALLERY OF ART, WASHINGTON

Sometimes cousins live close to you.

JOHN SINGER SARGENT "SIR NEVILLE WILKINSON ON THE STEPS OF A VENETIAN PALAZZO"
COURTESY NATIONAL GALLERY OF ART, WASHINGTON

39

And sometimes far away.

JOHN JACOB FREY "SUNRISE"
COURTESY NATIONAL GALLERY OF ART, WASHINGTON

41

Cousins are almost like sisters and brothers.

They have the same Grandma and Grandpa.

IPPOLITO CAFFI "INTERIOR OF THE COLOSSEUM"
COURTESY NATIONAL GALLERY OF ART, WASHINGTON

43

Best of all, when you grow up,

Your cousins will still be your cousins

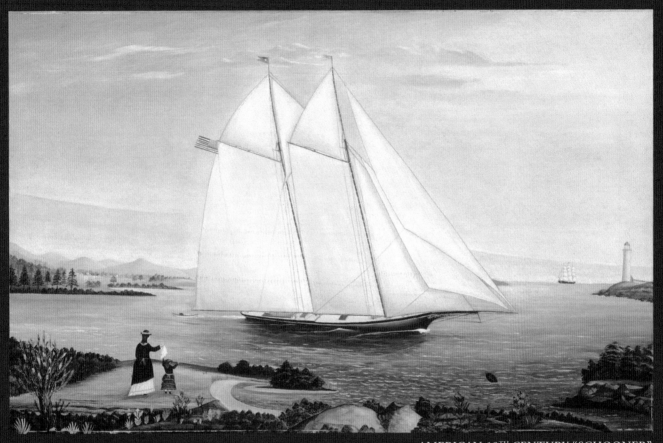

AMERICAN 19TH CENTURY "SCHOONER"
COURTESY OF THE NATIONAL GALLERY OF ART

Forever.

CLAUDE MONET "THE JAPANESE FOOTBRIDGE"
COURTESY OF THE NATIONAL GALLERY OF ART

47